BUSH VIPER

By Rachel Rose

Minneapolis, Minnesota

Credits
Cover and title page, © Mark Kostich/iStock; 3, © Mark Kostich/iStock; 4–5, © Mark Kostich/iStock; 6–7, © bennytrapp/Adobe Stock; 8, © Mark Kostich/iStock; 9, © Mark Kostich/iStock; 10–11, © bennytrapp/Adobe Stock; 12, © Mark Kostich/iStock; 13, © Roger de la Harpe/Adobe Stock; 14–15, © Mark Kostich/iStock; 16, © Mark Kostich/iStock; 17, © Henk Bogaard/iStock; 18–19, © Mark Kostich/Adobe Stock; 21, © Mark Kostich/iStock; 22T, © Leontura/iStock; 22B, © artemstepanov/Adobe Stock; 23, © Mark Kostich/iStock.

Bearport Publishing Company Product Development Team
President: Jen Jenson; Director of Product Development: Spencer Brinker; Managing Editor: Allison Juda; Associate Editor: Naomi Reich; Associate Editor: Tiana Tran; Art Director: Colin O'Dea; Designer: Kayla Eggert; Product Development Assistant: Owen Hamlin

STATEMENT ON USAGE OF GENERATIVE ARTIFICIAL INTELLIGENCE
Bearport Publishing remains committed to publishing high-quality nonfiction books. Therefore, we restrict the use of generative AI to ensure accuracy of all text and visual components pertaining to a book's subject. See BearportPublishing.com for details.

Library of Congress Cataloging-in-Publication Data

Names: Rose, Rachel, 1968- author.
Title: Bush viper / by Rachel Rose.
Description: Minneapolis, Minnesota : Bearport Publishing Company, [2025] | Series: Library of awesome animals | Includes bibliographical references and index.
Identifiers: LCCN 2023059635 (print) | LCCN 2023059636 (ebook) | ISBN 9798892320191 (library binding) | ISBN 9798892324977 (paperback) | ISBN 9798892321440 (ebook)
Subjects: LCSH: Atheris--Juvenile literature. | Snakes--Juvenile literature.
Classification: LCC QL666.O69 R669 2025 (print) | LCC QL666.O69 (ebook) | DDC 597.96/3--dc23/eng/20240129
LC record available at https://lccn.loc.gov/2023059635
LC ebook record available at https://lccn.loc.gov/2023059636

Copyright © 2025 Bearport Publishing Company. All rights reserved. No part of this publication may be reproduced in whole or in part, stored in any retrieval system, or transmitted in any form or by any means, electronic, mechanical, photocopying, recording, or otherwise, without written permission from the publisher. Bearport Publishing is a division of Chrysalis Education Group.

For more information, write to Bearport Publishing, 5357 Penn Avenue South, Minneapolis, MN 55419.

Contents

Awesome Bush Vipers! 4
Do Not Disturb 6
Spiky Dragons..................... 8
Slithering Snakes 10
That's a Wrap 12
Sharp Fangs, Deadly Venom 14
Danger Alert 16
Baby Time..................... 18
Ready, Set, Hunt! 20

Information Station 22
Glossary 23
Index 24
Read More 24
Learn More Online............................. 24
About the Author............................. 24

AWESOME
Bush Vipers!

SSS! A bush viper waits for its **prey** high up in a tree. The snake's colorful, pointy scales help it hide until it's ready to strike. Spiky masters of **camouflage**, bush vipers are awesome!

A BUSH VIPER'S **UNIQUE** SCALES ARE OFTEN LEAF-SHAPED, WITH RAISED CENTERS AND POINTED EDGES.

Do Not Disturb

A viper is a **venomous** snake. There are about 18 **species** of bush vipers throughout the warm regions of western and central Africa.

These snakes are **solitary** creatures, living alone in their rainforest and grassland **habitats**. But bush vipers don't just slither along on the ground. As their name suggests, they live in trees and thick bushes.

BUSH VIPERS ARE THE ONLY VENOMOUS SNAKES IN AFRICA THAT LIVE IN TREES.

Spiky Dragons

Many bush vipers are green to blend in with their planty homes. Their unique scales help them hide among the leaves, too. But spiky scales make bush vipers stand out in the world of **reptiles**. Some say the scales make these snakes look like dragons. The spiny bush viper is even nicknamed dragon bush viper. *RAWR!*

BUSH VIPERS CAN BE MANY DIFFERENT COLORS. THEY ARE GREEN, YELLOW, ORANGE, RED, OR EVEN BLUE.

A spiny bush viper

Slithering Snakes

Bush vipers have flat, wide heads and thin bodies. This lets the dragon-like snakes slither easily between the tight spaces in the branches of trees and bushes. Like all snakes, they move by using strong muscles attached to many ribs running along the length of their bodies.

Special scales on a snake's belly, called ventral scutes (VEN-truhl skootz), help the snake grip branches as it goes.

That's a Wrap

In addition to being expert climbers, these slithering snakes are excellent hunters, though the way they do it might look pretty relaxed. When it's time to find a meal, bush vipers mostly just hang out—literally. These snakes wrap their strong tails tightly around the branch of a bush or tree and wait from the hanging position.

BUSH VIPERS HUNT AT NIGHT. THEY HAVE LARGE EYES WITH SLIT PUPILS THAT OPEN WIDE IN THE DARK.

Pupil

Sharp Fangs, Deadly Venom

Bush vipers feed mostly on small mammals, birds, and reptiles. Once prey gets close, a bush viper strikes in a surprise attack. **WHAM!** The snake grabs the small animal in its mouth and bites down hard. Sharp, hollow fangs inject venom that quickly spreads throughout the victim's body. Once the venom has killed the creature, dinner is served.

Danger Alert

Though they are fierce **predators**, bush vipers can sometimes become prey. Luckily, their camouflage also keeps them hidden from animals that may want to eat them. Bush vipers hide from other snakes and large birds that seek them out for a tasty meal.

WHEN IN DANGER, A BUSH VIPER WILL MAKE A LOUD HISSING SOUND.

A black-chested snake eagle

Baby Time

Once a year when it's time to **mate**, bush vipers look for others. **Male** bush vipers will sway their heads from side to side to attract **females**. Depending on the species, female bush vipers give birth anywhere from two to seven months later. They can have up to 12 babies at once.

A baby bush viper

RATHER THAN LAYING EGGS AS MANY SNAKES DO, BUSH VIPERS GIVE BIRTH TO LIVE YOUNG.

Ready, Set, Hunt!

The female bush viper leaves her little babies, called snakelets, right away. Even though the snakelets are only about 6 inches (15 cm) long, they already have fangs filled with venom. Young bush vipers are ready to hunt and take care of themselves from the moment they are born. Now that's awesome!

BUSH VIPERS CAN LIVE FOR UP TO 20 YEARS.

Information Station

BUSH VIPERS ARE AWESOME!
LET'S LEARN MORE ABOUT THEM.

Kind of animal: Bush vipers are reptiles. Like all reptiles, they are cold-blooded, have scaly skin, and use lungs to breathe.

Other vipers: There are more than 200 species of vipers on Earth. Each of these snakes has fangs that inject venom into their prey.

Size: Most kinds of bush vipers can grow up to about 2.5 feet (0.7 m) long. That's about as long as an adult's arm.

BUSH VIPERS AROUND THE WORLD

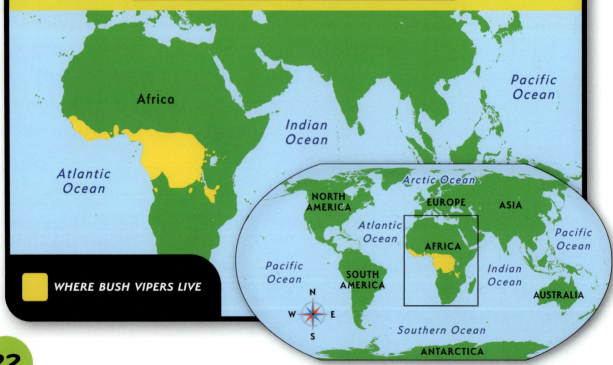

WHERE BUSH VIPERS LIVE

Glossary

camouflage patterns and colors on an animal's body that help it blend in with surroundings

females bush vipers that can give birth to young

habitats places in nature where animals live

male a bush viper that cannot give birth to young

mate to come together in order to have young

predators animals that hunt and kill other animals for food

prey an animal that is hunted and eaten by other animals

reptiles cold-blood animals that have dry, scaly skin and use lungs to breathe

solitary living alone

species groups that animals are divided into according to similar characteristics

unique uncommon or unusual

venomous full of poison that can be injected through fangs

Index

Africa 6, 22
camouflage 4, 16
fangs 14, 20, 22
female 18, 20
habitat 6
hunt 12, 20
male 18
mate 18
predator 16
prey 4, 14–16, 22
scales 4–5, 8, 11
snakelets 20
venom 6, 14, 20, 22

Read More

Davies, Monika. *Deadly Vipers (Deadly Snakes).* New York: Gareth Stevens Publishing, 2023.

Huddleston, Emma. *How Snakes Slither (The Science of Animal Movement).* Minneapolis: Abdo Publishing, 2021.

Learn More Online

1. Go to **www.factsurfer.com** or scan the QR code below.
2. Enter "**Bush Viper**" into the search box.
3. Click on the cover of this book to see a list of websites.

About the Author

Rachel Rose writes books for kids and teaches yoga. Her favorite animal for all time is her dog, Sandy.